Social Media Marketing Automation: How to Grow Your Brand Using Free AI Tools

(A Practical Guide to Streamlining Content, Engagement & Growth Without Spending Money)

By Andy Hai Dinh

This book is a work of nonfiction. While every effort has been made to ensure the accuracy of the information contained herein, the author makes no warranties regarding the completeness or applicability of the content. The tools, apps, and platforms referenced may change over time, and readers are encouraged to verify current features and terms of use.

For permissions, inquiries, or bulk purchases, contact:
haivdinh@gmail.com

TABLE OF CONTENTS

PREFACE
7

PART I — FOUNDATIONS
17

Chapter 1 — The New Era of Social Media Marketing
27

Chapter 2 — Understanding Social Media Ecosystems (Practical Mode)
39

Chapter 3 — The Automation Mindset (System Building)
51

PART II — THE FREE AI TOOLBOX
59

Chapter 4 — The Free AI Tools You'll Use
62

Chapter 5 — Setting Up Your AI Workspace
79

PART III — CONTENT AUTOMATION SYSTEMS
86

Chapter 6 — The AI Content Machine Framework (Input → Process → Output)

90

Chapter 7 — Automating Content Ideas
100

Chapter 8 — Scriptwriting & Caption Automation
104

Chapter 9 — AI-Powered Visual Content
108

Chapter 10 — Short-Form Video Automation
111

Chapter 11 — Automating Repurposing (The 1→15 Method)

114

Chapter 12 — Automating Posting & Scheduling
117

PART IV — ENGAGEMENT & GROWTH AUTOMATION
120

Chapter 13 — Automating Engagement Without Feeling Robotic
124

Chapter 14 — AI for Community Management
131

Chapter 15 — AI CRM Setup (Free Tools Only)
135

Chapter 16 — Analytics Automation (Weekly Report SOP)
138

PART V — ADVANCED SYSTEMS
141

Chapter 17 — Building a Fully Automated Content Assembly Line
146

Chapter 18 — AI Automation for Personal Brands
161

Chapter 19 — AI Automation for Businesses
164

Chapter 20 — Scaling With Zero Budget
167

PART VI — TEMPLATES, PROMPTS & BLUEPRINTS
170

Chapter 21 — High-Performing Prompts Library (Copy-Paste Ready)
177

Chapter 22 — Ready-to-Use Posting Calendars
187

Chapter 23 — Execution Checklists
190

Chapter 24 — Troubleshooting Guide
192

Chapter 25: Master System Map — How All SOPs Connect
196

Chapter 26: The Complete AI Prompt Library
218

Chapter 27: The Social Media Automation Prompt Pact
234

AFTERWORD
253

APPENDICES
260

OTHER BOOKS BY THIS AUTHOR
279

PREFACE

Social media has become the new marketplace, the new résumé, the new storefront, and—for many businesses—the new lifeline. Yet the biggest challenge is no longer *whether* you should create content or be active on social media. The real challenge is:

How do you do it consistently, effectively, and affordably?

Most entrepreneurs, creators, and small teams struggle not because they lack ambition or ideas, but because content creation has become overwhelming. Platforms change weekly. Algorithms shift. New trends appear every 24 hours. And expectations—daily posts, videos, graphics, captions, engagement, analytics—keep rising.

It feels impossible to keep up.

This book was written to solve that problem.

Why This Book Exists

The promise of this book is simple: **To teach you how to build a reliable, repeatable content machine using only free AI tools.**

No software subscriptions.
No editing suites.
No expensive automation systems.
No agency retainers.
No marketing degree required.

Inside these pages, you'll learn how to build a fully functioning social media marketing system—from idea to post to analytics—powered by free apps and free tiers of popular tools.

You will learn how to:

- Generate endless content ideas using AI
- Write posts in your authentic voice
- Create high-quality visuals, graphics, and carousels
- Produce short-form videos without expensive equipment
- Repurpose content automatically and efficiently
- Schedule posts across platforms
- Automate community responses and FAQs
- Track performance and analyze results
- Scale your output without burning out
- Maintain consistency even when life gets busy

This is **not** a theory book. This is **not** a collection of generic "content tips." This is a **practical manual** for building and automating your marketing workflow—step by step.

By the time you finish, you will know exactly how to set up a complete social media engine that runs with minimal effort and produces maximum impact, even on a zero-dollar budget.

Who This Book Is For

This book serves anyone who needs social media to grow but doesn't want (or can't afford) to spend thousands on tools and outsourcing.

It is especially created for:

Solopreneurs juggling operations, sales, fulfillment—and desperately needing a system that saves time.

Small business owners who want visibility without hiring a whole marketing department.

Creators who need efficiency, consistency, and a clear strategy without paying for premium apps.

Marketing managers on a budget who must maximize output with minimal resources.

Agencies that want repeatable systems to deliver more value, faster, without increasing headcount.

Beginners who are overwhelmed by the complexity of social media and want a structured plan.

Experts and professionals who are tired of inconsistent posting and ready for a predictable workflow.

No matter your background, this book will give you the clarity, tools, and systems to turn social media from a stressful obligation into a streamlined, automated engine of growth.

How to Use This Book

This book is designed as both a training program and a long-term reference. Each part has a purpose, and when followed in order, they build a complete social media automation system.

Parts I–III: Foundations, Mindset & Tools

You'll learn the underlying principles, the AI-powered workflow, and how free tools fit together into a powerful content engine. This section creates the blueprint you'll use for the rest of the book.

Parts IV–V: System Implementation

Here is where you build the machine. These chapters give you step-by-step instructions to:

- Create content

- Automate repurposing
- Auto-schedule posts
- Organize your weekly workflow
- Track and analyze results
- Set up templates for long-term consistency

This is the "do this, then this, then this" part of the book.

Part VI: Prompts, Templates & Checklists

This is your toolbox. You'll return to it repeatedly. It contains:

- Ready-to-use AI prompts
- Content templates
- System checklists
- Posting calendars

- Troubleshooting guides
- Optimization frameworks

Think of it as your personal Social Media Automation Reference Library.

How Each Chapter Works

To help you apply what you learn immediately, every chapter ends with Action Steps—simple, practical tasks you can implement the same day.

By completing these tasks consistently, you will not just read the book... **you will build your entire social media system as you go.**

A Final Word Before You Begin

The goal of this book is not to turn you into a full-time content creator. The goal is to help you:

- Grow your brand
- Build trust
- Stay consistent
- Save time
- Reduce stress
- Make content creation simple
- Use automation to your advantage
- Unlock opportunities that only visibility can bring

Social media is powerful, but only when used strategically and sustainably.

With the help of free AI tools, what once required a team—or thousands of dollars per month—can now be done by anyone.

By the end of this book, you will have a complete, automated content system that works every week, even when you're busy, tired, traveling, or focused on growing your business.

Let's begin building your automated growth engine.

PART I — FOUNDATIONS

Introduction

Before you can build a powerful, automated social media machine, you need a clear understanding of the landscape you're operating in. Part I is your foundation—the strategic layer that makes everything else in this book not only possible, but effective and sustainable.

Most people try to improve their social media presence by focusing on tactics first. They ask:

- "What should I post?"
- "What's the best platform?"
- "How do I grow faster?"

But tactics change weekly. Algorithms shift. Trends fade.

What never changes are the principles, systems, and frameworks behind successful social media marketing.

Part I shows you exactly how modern social media works, how to think like a strategist, and how to leverage AI to build workflows that compound over time.

This section gives you the mindset, the map, and the operating system you'll use for the rest of the book.

Why Foundations Matter More Than Ever

The era of guessing, posting randomly, and manually doing everything is over. Social media has moved from "post when you feel inspired" to "run a predictable content engine." The creators and brands who win today aren't posting more—they're posting *smarter*. They're using leverage, automation, repurposing, and AI to amplify their voice without increasing their workload.

When you understand the foundations, you stop:

- Wasting time on low-impact tasks
- Posting content that doesn't align with your brand
- Feeling overwhelmed by platform changes
- Chasing trends without strategy
- Burning out trying to "be everywhere"

Instead, you begin:

- Building systems that run on their own
- Producing content more consistently with less effort
- Using AI to speed up writing, scripting, visuals, and repurposing
- Creating a recognizable brand message
- Growing across platforms with one core workflow
- Making data-driven decisions
- Achieving more output while protecting your energy

This is the creator's advantage in the AI era. And you're about to master it.

What You'll Learn in Part I

Part I consists of three chapters, each one building on the previous to give you a complete understanding of how social media really works today.

Chapter 1 — The New Era of Social Media Marketing

You'll learn how the landscape has changed, why manual posting is no longer enough, and how AI reshapes every stage of content creation. You'll explore the four principles that top marketers follow: systems over one-offs, leverage over labor, human voice supported by AI, and automation that enhances relationships instead of replacing them.

By the end:

You'll have clarity on your core message, your audience's pain points, and your first 30-day platform focus.

Chapter 2 — Understanding Social Media Ecosystems (Practical Mode)

You'll dive into what each major platform prioritizes—short videos, long-form thought leadership, discoverability, community, or commentary—and learn exactly where automation can accelerate your workflow. You'll finally understand what belongs where, so your energy goes to the right content on the right platform.

By the end:

You'll have a mapped-out distribution plan for each platform you use, and clarity on how each piece of content will be repurposed.

Chapter 3 — The Automation Mindset (System Building)

This chapter teaches you to think like a content operator, not a content reactor. You'll learn the end-to-end editorial cycle used by top creators and agencies, as well as how to choose a sustainable posting cadence for 90 days—a timeframe proven to build momentum and consistency.

By the end:

You'll have your editorial cycle documented and a posting cadence you can maintain even on your busiest weeks.

How to Use Part I

Think of **Part I** as the blueprint. Before you build a house, you architect the structure. Before you automate your content machine, you define how it will work.

Throughout these chapters, you will be asked to:

- Make decisions
- Clarify your message
- Outline your system
- Choose a focus
- Document your workflow
- Apply what you learn immediately

Each chapter ends with **Action Steps** so that by the time you finish **Part I**, you aren't just informed—you're operational.

You will know:

- What you stand for
- Who you serve
- How to communicate your value
- How each platform works

- What your workflow looks like
- How AI will support you
- What cadence you'll follow
- How everything connects into one unified system

This foundation ensures that when you reach **Parts IV** and **V**—the implementation and automation sections—you can plug in each step without confusion or rework.

A Final Note Before You Begin

You don't need to be a tech expert, a designer, a writer, or a seasoned marketer to automate your content. You just need a framework that makes sense, a strategy that fits your goals, and tools that work for you instead of overwhelming you.

Part I is where clarity begins. It sets the direction, aligns your message, and prepares your systems. Once this foundation is solid, every piece of automation and AI support you add later becomes exponentially more powerful.

Let's build your content engine from the ground up—so it runs smoothly, consistently, and automatically.

Chapter 1 — The New Era of Social Media Marketing

Social media has undergone a dramatic transformation. What used to be a simple place to share updates with friends has become an ever-moving, hypercompetitive marketplace where attention is the currency and consistency is the cost of entry. The creators and brands that are winning today aren't doing more—they're doing **smarter**, and they're using systems and AI to do it.

This chapter explains the major shift happening across all platforms and breaks down the key principles that define modern social media success.

1.1 The Shift

When Manual Posting Worked

There was a time when social media success was simple:

- Snap a picture
- Write a caption
- Post it
- Hope people see it

That era is gone.

Platforms like Instagram, Facebook, and YouTube were once chronological. When you posted, your audience saw it. The competition was low. The algorithms were forgiving. "Post consistently" meant "share something every week or two."

Today's Reality: A Content Economy

Today, social media platforms are **entertainment engines powered by algorithms**, not chronological feeds. They reward:

- Frequency
- Relevance
- Engagement quality
- Retention
- Multi-format storytelling
- Timely reactions to trends
- Cross-platform consistency

Trying to do all this manually is nearly impossible without sacrificing sleep or sanity.

Why Systems Are the Modern Superpower

The successful creators aren't winging it. They rely on:

- Templates
- Repurposing frameworks
- Batch-creation sessions
- Content calendars
- AI-assisted idea generation
- Automated scheduling
- Documented workflows

What used to take a full-time team can now be done by a single person **with the right systems and AI tools**.

AI: The Great Friction Remover

AI does not replace creativity. AI replaces the *friction preventing creativity*.

It accelerates:

- **Ideation** — generate hooks, ideas, topics instantly
- **Writing** — turn rough notes into polished drafts
- **Editing** — rewrite, shorten, clarify, expand
- **Repurposing** — turn one piece of content into 10 formats
- **Formatting** — captions, scripts, outlines, descriptions
- **Research** — hashtags, keywords, angles, data points

AI removes the bottlenecks that used to make content creation slow, stressful, and inconsistent. When the friction disappears, consistency becomes natural.

1.2 Key Principles of the New Era

Principle 1: Systems Over One-Offs

Posting random content is not a strategy. You need **reliable workflows** —Standard Operating Procedures (SOPs)—that ensure:

- Ideas flow constantly
- Posts are created efficiently
- Editing is streamlined
- Scheduling is consistent
- Repurposing is automatic
- Measurement is routine

A system is a repeatable process you can execute even when life gets busy.

If you can't execute your social media plan on your busiest week, it's not a system—it's wishful thinking.

Principle 2: Leverage > Labor

In the old world, more effort = more output. In the AI world, more *leverage* = more output.

High-leverage content includes:

- Long-form videos
- Long-form posts
- Podcast episodes
- Training clips
- Articles
- Live streams
- Interviews

These long-form pieces can be sliced into:

- 10+ short videos
- 5–10 quote graphics
- 3–5 carousel posts
- 3–7 tweets
- A LinkedIn post
- A YouTube Short
- A blog post
- An email newsletter

One high-value piece of content becomes an entire week's output.

Principle 3: Human Voice + AI Scale

AI gives you structure, speed, and draft-quality content. But AI alone cannot replace **your voice, your story, your conviction, your tone**.

The winning formula is:

AI drafts → You refine → You publish at scale

You maintain the authenticity; AI accelerates the process.

Use AI to:

- Produce outlines
- Draft captions
- Suggest scroll-stopping hooks
- Create frameworks
- Provide variations

Then rewrite with:

- Your tone
- Your humor
- Your context
- Your lived experience

AI is the engine. You are the driver.

Principle 4: Automate the Routine, Own the Relationships

Automation should handle:

- FAQs
- "Link please?" type messages
- Appointment scheduling links
- Initial DM responses
- Comment routing
- Lead qualification

- Basic customer support

But **relationships**—trust, empathy, connection—can never be fully automated.

Humans respond to:

- Emotion
- Stories
- Personality
- Reputation
- Insight
- Vulnerability

AI handles the routine. You handle the relational.

This combination is unbeatable.

Action Steps

1. **Write down your brand's 3 core messages.**
   (What should you be known for?)

2. **Write down 3 major pain points your audience experiences.**
   (Why do they need you?)

3. **Choose ONE platform to focus on for the next 30 days.**
   Master one before expanding.

Chapter 2 — Understanding Social Media Ecosystems (Practical Mode)

Social media platforms behave like different cities—each with its own culture, language, and expectations. Trying to treat every platform the same is like showing up in Tokyo and expecting everyone to speak Italian.

This chapter breaks down what each platform rewards, how content spreads, and where automation can help you maximize your output without increasing your workload.

2.1 Platform Priorities

Instagram / TikTok: Visual & Fast-Paced

These platforms reward:

- Short-form videos
- Quick hooks
- High watch time
- Fast information
- Strong visuals
- Personality and authenticity
- Trends

Best for:

- Brand awareness
- Getting discovered
- Showing personality
- Storytelling

- Visual tutorials

Content formats:

- Reels / TikToks
- Carousels
- Short memes
- POVs
- Behind-the-scenes

LinkedIn: Depth & Professional Insight

LinkedIn rewards:

- Long-form thought leadership
- Professional frameworks
- Personal career stories
- Data-backed insights

- Business tips
- Authority and clarity

Best for:

- B2B businesses
- Coaches
- Agencies
- Consultants
- Corporate roles

Formats:

- Long-form posts
- Documents
- Articles
- Carousels
- Video explainers

YouTube: Discoverability & Long-Form Depth

YouTube is the only platform where content lives forever. A video posted today can still go viral 3 years later.

YouTube rewards:

- High watch time
- Strong retention
- High-value education
- Evergreen topics
- Consistency

Best for:

- Deep teachings
- Tutorials
- Reviews

- Stories
- Interviews
- How-tos

Formats:

- Long-form videos
- Shorts
- Playlists
- Livestreams

A single 10-minute video can be repurposed into:

- 3–7 Shorts
- Carousels
- Quotes
- Tweets
- Emails

- Blog posts

Facebook: Community & Conversation

Facebook rewards:

- Group activity
- Replies
- Comments
- Personal stories
- Lives
- Local content

Best for:

- Local businesses
- Coaches
- Community-driven niches

- Older audiences
- Broad markets

Formats:

- Group posts
- Lives
- Stories
- Reels
- Events

X (Twitter): Speed & Commentary

X rewards:

- Opinions
- News reactions
- Short statements

- Controversial takes
- One-liners
- Micro-insights

Best for:

- Thought leadership
- Tech
- Entrepreneurship
- Trends
- News commentary

Formats:

- Tweets
- Threads
- Quote tweets
- Memes

- Short videos

2.2 Where Automation Helps

Automation doesn't replace your creativity—it amplifies it and removes repetitive labor.

Where AI & Automation Improve Workflow

- Idea generation: endless hooks, topics, scripts
- Caption writing: polished, structured drafts
- Hashtag research: data-driven suggestions
- Scheduling: post across platforms automatically

- Repurposing: turn one video into 10 pieces
- Transcribing: convert speech to text instantly
- Reporting: weekly or monthly summaries
- Auto-responses: FAQ replies, DM filters, lead routing

Use AI heavily for efficiency. Use human judgment for creativity.

Action Steps

1. Map your content across platforms.

Example:

- TikTok + Reels → Short videos
- LinkedIn → Long-form articles

- YouTube → Long-form tutorials
- Facebook → Group conversations

2. Decide which platforms get repurposed content and which get original content.

Chapter 3 — The Automation Mindset (System Building)

Before you can automate anything, you need to think like the operator of a system—not the creator scrambling to keep up. This chapter teaches you the mindset and structure behind a sustainable social media workflow.

3.1 The Editorial Cycle

Every successful content machine follows a cycle. The amateur posts whenever inspiration strikes. The professional follows a documented process.

The full cycle:

1. Idea Harvest

Collect ideas daily through:

- AI prompts
- Customer questions
- Competitor research
- Comments
- Trends
- Books
- Podcasts

You don't need perfect ideas. You need *volume*.

2. Draft

Turn ideas into:

- Scripts

- Headlines
- Frameworks
- Outlines

AI can produce 70–80% of your drafts.

3. Visuals / Video

Create the media using:

- CapCut
- Canva
- Your smartphone
- Screen recordings
- Stock libraries
- Templates

Batch creation works best here.

4. Edit

Apply light editing:

- Trim videos
- Polish captions
- Add branding
- Add subtitles
- Standardize formatting

AI helps refine the copy; you oversee quality.

5. Publish

Use scheduling tools to distribute across:

- Instagram
- TikTok
- Facebook

- LinkedIn
- YouTube
- X

You should rarely publish manually.

6. Repurpose

Turn one core piece into:

- Shorts
- Carousels
- Quote graphics
- Threads
- Emails
- Blog posts

Repurposing multiplies your reach.

7. Analyze

Measure:

- Best posts
- Retention patterns
- Watch-time trends
- Topic performance
- Questions asked in comments

Then feed this data back into the idea stage.

This cycle is the heart of your entire content machine.

3.2 Choose a Cadence

Consistency beats intensity. Your cadence must match your lifestyle—not your ideal self.

Example realistic cadence:

- **3 posts per week**
  - 1 long-form (LinkedIn post or YouTube video)
  - 2 short-form (TikToks/Reels/Shorts)
- **Daily stories** (easy, low-effort)
- **Weekly engagement time**
  - 10–20 minutes replying to comments and DMs
- **Monthly long-form video or livestream**
  - Repurpose heavily afterward

If you try to post 3–5 times per day on every platform, you will burn out in two weeks.

If you post 3–5 times per week using systems and AI, you will grow consistently for years.

Action Steps

1. **Choose your 90-day cadence:** What can you commit to even during your busiest month?
2. **Write it down and save it as a weekly checklist.**
3. **Block 1–2 sessions per week for batch creation.**

PART II — THE FREE AI TOOLBOX

Introduction

Social media marketing used to require a full tech stack, expensive design software, and paid automation platforms. Not anymore. Today, you can build an entire content machine—from ideas to videos to analytics—using nothing but **free AI tools** and the free tiers of popular platforms. The purpose of **Part II** is to show you exactly *which* tools to use, *why* they matter, and *how* to set them up so they work together as a unified system.

Before we dive in, it's important to understand one thing: **free tiers evolve constantly.** Features shift, limits change, and new players appear. That's why this section focuses on *patterns* rather than brand loyalty. If one tool becomes paid-only, you'll know exactly how to replace it with an equivalent free option. You're not learning tools—you're learning **capabilities**: generating ideas, drafting content, designing visuals, editing videos, scheduling, automating workflows, and tracking performance.

Think of this toolbox as your command center. In the next chapters, you'll get:

- Short, practical setup steps for each tool
- The first three actions to take to start seeing results immediately
- Templates for your workspace structure
- SOPs (standard operating procedures) that turn every tool into a repeatable workflow

You don't need to master everything at once. In the beginning, simply choose the tools that match your content type—text, images, or videos—and gradually expand your toolkit as your workflow becomes smoother. By the end of this part, you'll have a fully functional AI-powered workspace capable of supporting consistent content creation, smart automation, and hands-free scheduling.

Let's build your toolbox—piece by piece—and turn free AI into your competitive advantage.

Chapter 4 — The Free AI Tools You'll Use

A practical guide to setup, first steps, and smart usage patterns

Free AI tools are the backbone of your automated social media system. You don't need fancy subscriptions or premium upgrades—you just need the right combination of text generators, image tools, video editors, and automators. This chapter walks you through each category, gives you a simple setup, and hands you the exact first three steps to take so you're productive immediately. Please complete the setup and the first 3 actions for each tool as you read along.

4.1 TEXT & STRATEGY TOOLS

ChatGPT (Free Tier)

Primary use: brainstorming, content ideas, caption writing, scripts, outlines, and prompt storage.

Why it matters:

ChatGPT is your *creative engine*. It turns your raw ideas into structured posts and gives you multiple versions of any piece of content. The goal isn't to copy/paste blindly—it's to build fast, consistent first drafts that you refine into your brand voice.

Setup (1 paragraph):

Sign in and create a dedicated document (Notion, Google Docs, or a simple Notes app) called **Brand**

Prompts. This becomes your personal library of prompts you'll use repeatedly —hooks, scripts, captions, repurposing prompts, and engagement prompts. Keeping them in one place ensures consistency and eliminates the need to start from scratch every time.

First 3 Actions:

1. Paste your **3 core brand messages** and **3 audience pain points** into a single reference prompt.
2. Ask: ***"Generate 30 content ideas based on these."***
3. Ask: ***"Give me 5 strong hooks for a social post."***

Google Gemini / Perplexity / Claude (Free Tiers)

Primary use: alternate phrasing, fact-checking, idea expansion, and cross-referencing.

Why it matters:
Different AIs think differently. Cross-checking ideas across 2–3 models gives you more variety, fewer repetitive phrases, and more confidence in accuracy (especially for educational content).

Setup:

Create a bookmark folder labeled **AI Assistants** and store all AI tools there. Log into each once so history and preferences save.

First 3 Actions:

1. Ask for **10 alternate angles** of one content idea ChatGPT generated.
2. Fact-check one claim in your niche.

3. Ask for **3 rewrites** of a caption in different tones (casual, professional, bold).

Notion (Free)

Primary use: your command center—content calendar, asset links, brand hub, prompts, SOPs, CRM, and analytics notes.

Setup:

Create a page called **Content HQ**. Inside, add one database called **Content Items** with the fields: Title, Platform, Status, Publish Date, Content Type, Assets Links, AI Prompt Used, Repurpose List, Performance Notes.

First 3 Actions:

1. Create 5 content cards with tentative topics.

2. Link placeholder assets (even if empty for now).
3. Create a subpage called **Brand Prompts** and paste your prompt library.

4.2 IMAGE & DESIGN TOOLS

Canva (Free)

Primary use: designing carousels, reels covers, thumbnails, quote posts, infographics, and templates.

Setup:

Create a free account and immediately go to **Brand Kit** to upload your logo (if you have one), set your brand colors, and choose 1–2 fonts. This ensures instant uniformity and cuts design time by 70%.

First 3 Actions:

1. Build three post templates:

   - Quote
   - Tips list
   - Carousel (3–5 slides)

2. Export them into your **/Assets/Images/Templates** folder.

3. Add your brand colors and fonts into the "Styles" panel for instant reuse.

<u>Bing Image Creator / DALL·E-lite / Stable Diffusion (Free UIs)</u>

Primary use: concept visuals, abstract backgrounds, object photos, modern thumbnails, stylized graphics.

Setup:

Open the tool and create a folder called **Generated Images** under your Assets directory. Decide on your preferred visual style—minimalist, bold, cinematic, cartoon, or photorealistic—and save your prompt formulas.

First 3 Actions:

1. Generate an image for one of your content ideas ("minimalist background for carousel," "modern digital marketing icon," etc.).
2. Download low-resolution version (good enough for social).
3. Upload it into Canva and use it as the base for a design.

4.3 VIDEO & SHORT-FORM TOOLS

CapCut (Free App/Web)

Primary use: trimming, automatic captions, transitions, B-roll, templates, voice effects.

Setup:

Install the app (or use the web editor) and create a preset project with your brand font, caption style, and typical colors. This acts as your auto-brand video template.

First 3 Actions:

1. Import a short clip and test auto-captions.
2. Apply one template and export a 9:16 video.
3. Save the project as **Brand Template** for future videos.

VEED / InVideo (Free)

Primary use: subtitles, trimming, basic effects, fast editing in the browser.

Setup:

Create a free account, choose one editor as your backup tool. Bookmark both in case one limits features later.

First 3 Actions:

1. Upload a raw vertical clip.
2. Add subtitles using auto-caption.
3. Export and compare with CapCut results.

TikTok Creative Assistant (Free)

Primary use: trend detection, trending templates, sound suggestions, script ideas.

Setup:

Log in through the TikTok app or web version. Turn on notifications for trending formats.

First 3 Actions:

1. Search your niche and save 3 trending templates.
2. Use a template to generate one script.
3. Add it as an idea card in your **Notion Content HQ**.

4.4 SCHEDULING & AUTOMATION TOOLS

Buffer Free / Metricool Free

Primary use: schedule posts, store captions, preview feeds, and moderate comments (limited).

Setup:

Connect only the platforms you actively plan to publish on. Create separate queues for each platform (IG, TikTok, FB, LinkedIn).

First 3 Actions:

1. Schedule one post as a draft with a placeholder image.
2. Test posting to one platform.
3. Create your weekly posting slots (e.g., Tue–Thu 7AM).

Zapier Free / Make.com Free

Primary use: simple automation—move content, sync databases, send reminders, create drafts.

Setup:

Choose 1–2 "starter automations" only so your free task quota lasts. Examples:

- Notion → Buffer draft
- New Google Sheet entry → Slack reminder
- Google Drive file → Notion attachment

First 3 Actions:

1. Create one Zap/Scenario that moves a new Notion card into a Buffer draft.
2. Test it with fake content.
3. Document it in your SOPs.

IFTTT Free

Primary use: cross-posting and simple triggers (e.g., "New IG post → auto-share to Facebook").

Setup:

Browse the "Social" category and activate only automations you will genuinely use.

First 3 Actions:

1. Turn on a cross-post trigger.
2. Post a test piece of content.
3. Check if the automation worked correctly.

4.5 ANALYTICS & SPREADSHEETS

Google Sheets

Primary use: KPI tracking, performance logs, content audit, dashboard inputs.

Setup:

Create a sheet called **Content Performance Tracker** with columns for: Platform, Post Type, Publish Date, Views, Likes, Comments, Saves, Shares, Click-through Rate, Notes.

First 3 Actions:

1. Add your 3 most recent posts as entries.
2. Add conditional formatting for top 10% performance.
3. Write one insight about engagement patterns.

Google Data Studio (Looker Studio) Free

Primary use: Automated dashboards from Google Sheets.

Setup:

Connect your KPI Google Sheet as a data source. Create a "**Content Dashboard**" with bar charts for reach, line charts for growth, and tables for top performers.

First 3 Actions:

1. Create your first dashboard page.
2. Add 1–2 visualizations.
3. Set the dashboard to update automatically from Sheets.

Chapter 4 — Action Steps

- Sign up for every tool you plan to use.
- Create a master login list in Notion or 1Password.
- Build in Notion:
  - **Content Database**
  - **Brand Prompts** page
  - **Assets folder** (with subfolders: Images, Videos, Templates)

Chapter 5 — Setting Up Your AI Workspace

Your organized, automated content machine begins here

Most creators fail not because they lack ideas—but because their workflow is messy. If your files, prompts, videos, and drafts are scattered across 15 locations, you'll always feel behind.

This chapter gives you a clean, frictionless workspace that turns your content production into a replicable system.

5.1 Folder & Naming Conventions

You will create one master folder:

BrandName / SocialAutomation /

Inside it:

- **/Assets/**
  - /Images/
  - /Videos/
  - /Templates/
- **/Prompts/**
- **/SOPs/**
- **/Calendar/**
- **/Exports/** (optional but helpful)

This structure ensures everything has a home—and you never wonder where something lives.

Naming Convention:

Use this formula:

YYYY-MM-DD_Platform_ContentType_Descriptor_Version.ext

Examples:

- 2025-12-10_IG_Reel_HookHowTo_Short.mp4
- 2025-12-11_LI_Carousel_AIProductivity_v1.png
- 2025-12-12_TT_Script_BestHooks_v2.txt

This makes files sortable, searchable, and future-proof.

5.2 Notion Content Database Schema

Create a database with these fields:

- **Title**
- **Platform**
- **Content Type** (Reel, Post, Carousel, Tweet, YouTube Short, etc.)
- **Status** (Idea → Draft → In Review → Scheduled → Posted)
- **Publish Date**
- **AI Prompt Used**
- **Assets Links**
- **Repurpose List** (future variants)
- **Performance Notes**

This one database becomes your calendar, your strategy map, and your analytics log.

5.3 Starter SOPs (Standard Operating Procedures)

SOPs turn chaos into predictable output. Each SOP should be 5–15 steps and written like a checklist.

Start with these:

1. **Create a Short-Form Video**
2. **Repurpose Long-Form Video into 10 Clips**
3. **Weekly Analytics Report**

SOP Example — Create a Short-Form Video (CapCut + ChatGPT)

1. Run ChatGPT prompt:

"Given my brand voice {insert 3 lines}, generate 5 hooks for a 30–60 second reel about {topic}."

2. Pick 1 hook and ask ChatGPT for a script (30–45 seconds, three scenes, clear CTA).
3. Record footage on your phone (3 takes).
4. Upload raw footage to **/Assets/Videos/**.
5. Open CapCut:
   - Import clips
   - Auto-caption
   - Add B-roll
   - Apply Brand Template
6. Export two versions:
   - 9:16 (Reels, TikTok, Shorts)
   - 1:1 (Instagram feed)
     Save in **/Assets/Videos/**.
7. Use ChatGPT to write 3 caption variations + hashtags.

8. Upload as a draft to Buffer or Metricool.

Chapter 5 — Action Steps

- Build your full Notion schema.
- Add 5 content ideas into the database.
- Create folders + naming conventions in your storage system.
- Write your first SOP.

PART III — CONTENT AUTOMATION SYSTEMS

Introduction

Content is no longer about posting when you feel creative. It's about building a **machine**—a predictable, repeatable, AI-assisted engine that turns your ideas into consistent output across multiple platforms. The goal of this section is to teach you how to think, operate, and execute like a streamlined digital publisher—even if you're a one-person business, a creator on a budget, or a marketing manager with limited time.

In earlier parts of this book, you learned the foundations and built your toolbox. Now we bring everything together into a **fully functioning automation system**. The chapters in Part III walk you through how to turn raw ideas into finished content, how to use AI to multiply each piece of content into many formats, and how to automate parts of your workflow so your content ecosystem runs smoothly—even when you're busy, offline, or focused on higher-level strategy.

Think of this part as the "operating manual" for your content machine. Every system (ideas, scripts, visuals, videos, repurposing, scheduling) is broken down into clear frameworks, SOPs, prompts, and step-by-step workflows you can immediately apply. You'll learn how to:

- Capture and organize every idea instantly
- Expand ideas into scripts, captions, and carousels with AI
- Automate thumbnails, visuals, and video workflows

- Repurpose one long piece of content into many smaller ones
- Build a cross-platform publishing schedule
- Set up automations that reduce your workload every week

The systems here are designed to save you hours, eliminate decision fatigue, and help you maintain consistency—which is the real currency of digital growth.

At the end of every chapter, you'll find **Action Steps** so you can apply what you learn immediately. By the time you finish **Part III**, you will have a fully operational content machine that you can run in just a few hours per week.

Content automation is the engine that separates creators who "post when inspired" from creators who publish consistently, strategically, and at scale.

In this part, you will build a system that transforms a single raw idea into a full ecosystem of posts across multiple platforms—without burning out or reinventing the wheel each time.

AI is not here to replace creativity. It's here to multiply it.

Let's turn your ideas into an automated engine for growth.

Chapter 6 — The AI Content Machine Framework (Input → Process → Output)

How to systemize idea capture, AI processing, and multi-platform output.

6.1 Understanding Inputs: The Fuel of Your Content Machine

Every piece of content begins with an input. Most creators fail not because they lack creativity, but because they lack captured creativity. An idea that is not captured is an idea that is lost forever.

What Counts as Inputs?

Inputs are any raw materials you feed into the content machine:

- **Raw ideas** — random thoughts, shower ideas, insights from conversations
- **Long-form content** — podcasts, YouTube videos, livestreams, speeches, interviews
- **Written content** — newsletters, essays, articles
- **Customer questions** — comments, emails, DMs, FAQs
- **Field observations** — trends you see online, industry changes, competitor posts
- **Personal stories** — life lessons, failures, behind-the-scenes moments

Your Capture Rule: Every Idea Lives in One Place

Use Notion as your single source of truth.

Your rule:

If you think it, see it, or say it, it must be captured in Notion immediately.

Your Capture System (simple & fast)

1. Install Notion mobile widget.
2. Create a database called ***Content Inputs***.
3. Add fields: Topic / Platform / Notes / Tag / Status.

4. When an idea hit you → open widget → type 1 line → save.
5. Sort all ideas weekly and choose which enter the “Process” stage.

The goal:

You never start content creation from a blank page again.

6.2 Processing With AI (Step-by-Step Machine Assembly)

This is where raw inputs turn into structured content.

The rule: ***Batch your processing. Never create content one piece at a time.***

1. Idea Expansion (10 Ideas → 50 Micro-Ideas)

You feed ChatGPT 10 seed ideas and it expands them into 50.

Example workflow:

1. Gather 10 of your Notion ideas.
2. Paste into ChatGPT.
3. Use your expansion prompt (found in Part VI).
4. Save all micro ideas back into Notion with tags.

Result:

You always have more ideas than time.

2. Script Generation (AI First Draft → Human Polish)

Let AI generate:

- Hooks
- Outlines
- Scripts for short-form videos
- Carousel outlines
- Long posts

Your job is to:

- Add brand voice
- Add personal stories
- Add strong emotional language
- Remove robotic or repetitive phrasing

AI = speed
Human = soul

3. Visual Asset Generation

Use AI for early-stage ideation:

- ChatGPT for visual descriptions
- Bing Image Creator (or Midjourney) for concept mockups
- Canva templates for final execution
- Use your brand kit for consistency

Create a system where every video gets:

- 1 thumbnail
- 1 placeholder caption
- 1 folder of assets

4. Repurpose Plan (Your Content Multiplying System)

For every long-form piece (10–20 min video, podcast, livestream):

Create a Repurpose Sheet with:

- 5 Tweets / X posts
- 3 short videos
- 2 carousels
- 1 quote graphic

Result: One input → 11 outputs.

6.3 Output: Publishing & Repurposing

Once content is polished, it must be:

1. Posted
2. Repurposed
3. Re-distributed

Your workflow:

1. Publish the main piece.
2. Immediately trigger the repurpose workflow (**Chapter 11**).
3. Schedule micro-content across platforms.
4. Add "Published" or "Repurposed" status in Notion.

Action Steps

- Pick one input this week (a 10-minute video works great).
- Run it fully through the Input → Process → Output machine.
- Publish 1 piece, repurpose into 5 micro outputs.

Your content machine is now officially running.

Chapter 7 — Automating Content Ideas

7.1 Prompt Stacks for Idea Generation

This is your **Master Prompt**. Save it in Notion.

Master Prompt (copy/paste)

I am {brand_name}.
My voice: {3 adjectives}.
My audience: {audience description}.

Give me 30 content ideas for {platform} about {topic}.

For each idea include:
- 1-line hook

- Suggested format (short video, carousel, long post)
- Estimated length
- 3 supporting bullets
- Repurpose list (tweets, short clips, carousel slides, quotes)

Use this once per week to fill your pipeline.

7.2 Trend Monitoring (Free & Fast)

Trends give you angles, not topics.

Use:

- Instagram Reels "Trends"
- TikTok Discover
- YouTube Trending

- Google Trends
- Perplexity summaries

Process:

1. Save trend links or screenshots in Notion.
2. Write one sentence describing why the trend works.
3. Let AI turn that angle into 5–10 content ideas.

7.3 Competitor Intelligence (Ethical & Strategic)

You do not copy competitors—you study *why* their posts performed.

Workflow:

1. Screenshot or save link of a high-performing competitor post.

2. Paste into ChatGPT with:

Why did this post get high engagement?
Break down: hook, structure, psychology, CTA, timing.
Suggest a variant using my brand voice.

3. Save best variants as new ideas in Notion.

Action Steps

- Use the **Master Prompt** now to generate 30 ideas.
- Pick the best 10.
- Tag them "Ready for Script" in Notion.

Chapter 8 — Scriptwriting & Caption Automation

8.1 Script Formats (Your Plug-and-Play Models)

Short Hook Script (0–15s)

- Hook
- Problem
- Micro-solution
- CTA

Mini-Tutorial (30–60s)

- Hook
- Step 1
- Step 2

- Step 3
- Outcome
- CTA

Carousel Script (5 Slides)

- Slide 1: Title
- Slide 2: Problem
- Slides 3–4: Solution steps
- Slide 5: CTA

8.2 Prompt for Script Generation

Write a 45-second TikTok script in a conversational tone.
Hook: {hook}.

Include:

- Three short scenes
- Visual/cutaway suggestions
- Suggested captions for each scene
- CTA: "save this post" and "follow for more"

Keep all sentences under 12 words.

8.3 Caption & Hashtag Automation

Generate 3 caption variations for this script: short, medium, long.
Include 10 relevant hashtags.
Also generate a first pinned comment with 10 additional hashtags.

8.4 Scheduling for A/B Testing

To avoid noise:

- Change ONE variable per test:
  - Caption OR posting time

Use **Buffer's "variations" feature** to test two caption versions.

Action Steps

- Pick 3 ideas from Notion.
- Generate scripts, captions, hashtags.
- Upload into your scheduler.

Chapter 9 — AI-Powered Visual Content

9.1 Build a Reusable Brand Template in Canva

1. Open Canva → Create new 1080×1080 design.
2. Add brand colors, fonts, logo placement.
3. Create 5 templates:

- Quote
- Tip
- Stats
- Carousel title
- Carousel content slide

4. Save as reusable brand kit.
5. Duplicate for each new post.

9.2 Automating Thumbnails

Workflow:

1. Ask ChatGPT:

Give me 5 thumbnail headline ideas for this video.

2. Paste the best headline into your Canva thumbnail template.
3. Export as PNG.

This turns thumbnails into a 3–minute task.

9.3 Lightning-Fast Carousel Workflow

1. Generate outline in ChatGPT (8–10 points).
2. Paste outline into Canva "Create multiple pages."
3. Drag in 2–3 images.
4. Export carousel PNGs.

Action Steps

- Build one carousel template now.
- Create one sample post with it.

Chapter 10 — Short-Form Video Automation

10.1 Recording Best Practices

- Vertical 9:16
- Natural window light
- Use a $20 lapel mic
- Record 3–4 short takes
- Avoid busy backgrounds
- Never memorize scripts—use talking points

10.2 CapCut Editing SOP

1. Import clips.

2. Trim to 3 scenes.
3. Auto-generate captions → correct timing.
4. Add B-roll or overlays.
5. Export 1080×1920.

10.3 AI Voiceover & TTS

- Use CapCut or any free TTS generator.
- Choose one voice for consistency.
- Always spot-check pronunciation.

Action Steps

- Record 2 videos today.

- Edit in CapCut.
- Export vertical + 1:1 versions.

Chapter 11 — Automating Repurposing (The 1→15 Method)

11.1 Repurpose Map Example

From ONE 20-minute recording, produce:

- 1 long-form article
- 5 short-form vertical videos
- 6 tweets or X threads
- 3 carousels
- 5 stories

Total: 20-minute input → 15+ micro outputs

11.2 Repurpose SOP (Use ChatGPT)

Step-by-step:

1. Paste transcript into ChatGPT:

Split this transcript into 5 short scripts optimized for Reels. Add a hook and CTA.

2. Ask:

Create 6 tweet-sized quotes from this transcript.

3. Ask:

Write a LinkedIn summary + 3 carousel slide headings.

4. Create carousels in Canva.

11.3 Automating the Transcript

Use:

- CapCut (free auto caption)
- VEED (free)

Export transcript → upload to Notion.

Action Steps

- Take one long video.
- Generate 5–10 micro outputs.
- Schedule them.

Chapter 12 — Automating Posting & Scheduling

12.1 Buffer / Metricool Setup (Free)

1. Connect platforms:
   - Instagram
   - Facebook
   - Twitter/X
   - LinkedIn
2. Upload media assets.
3. Add captions.
4. Schedule posting:
   - IG: 4–6 weekly
   - TikTok: 3–5 weekly

- X/Twitter: Daily
- LinkedIn: 2–3 weekly

12.2 Zapier Automation (Free)

Example Zap: Notion → Buffer Draft

Trigger:

When Notion entry has Status = "Scheduled"

Action:

Create a Buffer draft:

- Caption
- Image link
- Platform

This removes 80% of manual posting.

12.3 Time Optimization With AI

Feed AI your weekly analytics:

Here are my last 7 days of engagement data.
Suggest optimal posting times for each platform.
Make a hypothesis schedule for me to test.

Action Steps

- Create one Zap: Notion → Buffer draft.
- Test with one scheduled post.

PART IV — ENGAGEMENT & GROWTH AUTOMATION

Introduction

Creating content is only half the game. Growth happens in the conversations that follow.

Likes and views may signal reach, but **engagement builds trust**, and trust is what turns followers into customers, clients, and advocates. The challenge is that as your content output increases, your ability to personally respond to every comment, message, and interaction becomes strained. This is where most creators either burn out—or disengage entirely.

Part IV exists to solve that problem.

In this section, you'll learn how to **automate engagement without losing humanity**. The goal is not to sound robotic, spammy, or impersonal. The goal is to use AI as a *support system*—drafting responses, organizing conversations, routing messages, and summarizing insights—while keeping humans in control of tone, empathy, and relationship depth.

You will build systems that allow you to:

- Respond faster and more consistently to comments and DMs
- Welcome new community members at scale
- Handle FAQs without repeating yourself
- Track leads and conversations using free tools
- Generate weekly engagement and growth insights automatically

The philosophy of this part is simple:

Automate the routine. Humanize the meaningful.

AI should handle first drafts, sorting, grouping, and reminders. Humans should handle nuance, emotion, judgment, and relationship building. When used correctly, automation doesn't distance you from your audience—it actually gives you *more time* to show up where it matters most.

Each chapter in this part includes:

- Clear SOPs you can reuse daily or weekly
- Ethical guidelines for automation
- Free-tool-only setups
- Action steps you can implement immediately

By the end of **Part IV**, you will have a scalable engagement system that feels personal, responsive, and aligned with your brand—without requiring you to be online 24/7.

Let's turn engagement into a growth engine—without burning out or sounding like a bot.

Chapter 13 — Automating Engagement Without Feeling Robotic

Automation should never replace connection. Its purpose is to remove delay, repetition, and cognitive load so can show up consistently with warmth and intention. This chapter shows you how to blend AI efficiency with human judgment.

13.1 Responding to Comments (Human + AI)

Comments are public conversations. How you respond shapes brand perception more than the original post.

The mistake most people make is either:

- Responding too slowly, or
- Copy-pasting robotic replies that kill authenticity

The solution is a draft-assist system.

The Comment Response SOP

Tools needed:

- Notion
- ChatGPT (free)

Step 1: Export comments daily

- At the end of each day, copy comments from posts into a Notion database.
- Fields to include:

- Date
- Platform
- Post link
- Comment text
- Comment type (Praise / Question / Objection / Sales Inquiry)
- Status (Drafted / Approved / Posted)

Step 2: Group by comment type

Create filters or tags so comments are grouped into:

- Praise (“This helped so much!”)
- Questions (“How do I do this?”)
- Objections (“Does this even work?”)
- Pricing / sales inquiries

Step 3: Use ChatGPT to draft replies

Paste grouped comments into ChatGPT using a structured prompt.

Example Prompt (Pricing Questions):

Create 10 short replies to comments asking about pricing.
Tone: helpful, calm, curious.
Avoid pushiness.
Include a soft CTA inviting them to DM for details.
Keep each reply under 25 words.

Step 4: Human review

- Adjust tone
- Add personal touches (names, emojis, specifics)
- Approve before posting

Rule: AI drafts. Humans approve. Always.

13.2 Auto-DMs (Use Sparingly)

Auto-DMs should open doors—not shove people through them.

When auto-DMs work well:

- New followers
- Lead magnets
- Simple keyword triggers (“guide”, “pricing”)

When they don’t:

- Complex questions
- Emotional messages

- Objections or complaints

Best Practice Setup

- Use platform-native tools first (Instagram Quick Replies, LinkedIn Saved Replies).
- Keep auto-DMs short and optional.

Example Auto-DM:

"Thanks for checking out my content! If you're curious about [topic], reply 'INFO' and I'll send details."

Once the user replies, route to a human.

Action Steps (Chapter 13)

- Create a Notion "Comment Response" database
- Write 10 canned replies (praise, pricing, FAQs)
- Train ChatGPT with your brand tone to generate variations

Chapter 14 — AI for Community Management

Communities grow when newcomers feel oriented and existing members feel supported. Automation ensures no one slips through the cracks.

14.1 Welcome Automation

A strong welcome message:

- Sets expectations
- Shares key resources
- Establishes tone

Pinned Welcome Message Template

Automate a pinned welcome message and a DM for new members (if platform allows) with links to resources.

Include:

1. Who the group is for
2. What members will learn
3. Where to start (links)
4. Community rules

Example:

"Welcome! Start with the pinned resources, introduce yourself, and feel free to ask questions. This is a learning-first space."

If the platform allows:

- Auto-DM new members with the same message

14.2 FAQ Handling with AI

Repetitive questions drain energy. FAQs reclaim time.

FAQ Knowledge Base SOP

Step 1: In Notion, list:

- Question
- Short answer (2–3 sentences)
- Link to deeper resource

Step 2: Use ChatGPT to rewrite answers into:

- One-sentence replies
- Friendly conversational tone

Step 3: Save these as:

- Quick replies
- Bot snippets
- Pinned FAQ cards

Action Steps (Chapter 14)

- Write one welcome message
- Create 5 FAQ answers in Notion
- Save them as platform quick replies

Chapter 15 — AI CRM Setup (Free Tools Only)

Most creators lose leads because conversations live in DMs and nowhere else.

Your CRM doesn't need to be complex —it needs to be used.

15.1 Notion as a CRM

Create a database with these fields:

- Lead Name
- Platform
- First Touch Date
- Interest Level (Cold / Warm / Hot)

- Tags (Service, Product, Inquiry Type)
- Next Step
- Conversation Snippets
- Last Contacted

This becomes your single source of truth.

15.2 DM Pipeline SOP

Step 1: Capture

- Every meaningful DM → add to Notion
- Tag as "New"

Step 2: Draft follow-ups with ChatGPT

Example Prompt:

Write three follow-up messages:
1) 30% interest check-in
2) 3-day follow-up
3) 7-day final follow-up
Tone: respectful, not salesy.

Step 3: Human sends

Never auto-send sales messages.

Action Steps (Chapter 15)

- Build a Notion CRM template
- Add 5 sample leads
- Draft a 3-message follow-up sequence

Chapter 16 — Analytics Automation (Weekly Report SOP)

Data is useless without interpretation. Automation turns numbers into decisions.

16.1 What to Track

Track weekly:

- Impressions
- Reach
- Engagement Rate
- Follower Growth
- Clicks

- Saves
- Shares
- Top 3 posts

16.2 Weekly Report SOP

Step 1: Export CSVs from platforms

Step 2: Paste into Google Sheets

Step 3: Use formulas for:

- Week-over-week % change
- Engagement rate

Step 4: Generate insight with ChatGPT

Prompt:

Given the following metrics, write:
• A 4-sentence performance summary
• 3 hypotheses for improvement next week

Action Steps (Chapter 16)

- Build a Google Sheet with labeled columns
- Create a formulas tab for % change

PART V — ADVANCED SYSTEMS

From Workflows to Machines

Advanced systems are not about doing more work. They are about **controlling flow**.

At this stage, your goal is no longer to "create content.

Your goal is to run an **assembly line** where content moves forward automatically, predictably, and with quality control.

Up to this point, you've learned how to automate individual pieces of the social media process—ideas, scripts, visuals, posting, engagement, and analysis.

Those systems alone can dramatically reduce effort and increase consistency.

But advanced operators don't think in parts.

They think in **pipelines**.

PART V is where everything clicks together. This section is about transforming scattered workflows into a **fully connected content machine**—one that runs with clarity, checkpoints, and accountability. Instead of asking, *"What should I post today?"* you'll know exactly where content enters the system, how it moves forward, and who (or what) is responsible at each stage.

This is the difference between:

- Posting when you have time
- And publishing because the system says it's time

Advanced systems remove emotion from execution. They make output predictable, quality controllable, and scale possible—without adding stress or cost.

What This Section Unlocks

In **PART V**, you will:

- Build an end-to-end content assembly line that prevents bottlenecks
- Separate creative judgment from mechanical execution
- Learn how personal brands and businesses use the same core system with different inputs
- Scale output without upgrading tools—or burning out

You'll stop managing tasks and start **operating a machine**.

Why This Matters

Most creators fail at scale not because they lack ideas—but because everything depends on them, all the time. Advanced systems introduce:

- Clear ownership
- Approval gates
- Repeatable output
- Reliable momentum

Once these systems are in place, growth becomes calm instead of chaotic.

Think of **PART V** as the moment your brand stops behaving like a hustle—and starts behaving like an operation.

Let’s build the machine.

Chapter 17 — Building a Fully Automated Content Assembly Line

This chapter turns chaos into a conveyor belt.

Most creators operate in reactive mode:

- Ideas live in their head
- Content gets created randomly
- Posting depends on motivation
- Engagement happens only when remembered

A content assembly line removes all of that friction.

Every piece of content enters at one end, passes through clearly defined stages, and exits as published content—without confusion, duplication, or burnout.

17.1 The End-to-End Pipeline

The pipeline is the backbone of your system.

Every step has:

- A **clear input**
- A **clear output**
- An **owner**
- A **checkpoint**

Nothing moves forward without approval.

Step 1: Idea Capture → Notion (Quick Capture)

Input:

- Raw ideas
- Voice notes
- Observations
- Questions from DMs
- Trends or competitor inspiration

Tool:

- Notion mobile app (Inbox or Ideas database)

SOP:

1. Create a Notion database called Content Inbox.

2. Fields:
   - Idea title
   - Source (Idea / Trend / DM / Client / Call)
   - Platform
   - Status (Inbox → Approved → In Production)
3. Capture ideas instantly—no filtering.

Checkpoint:

- Weekly review.
- Only ideas marked Approved move forward.

Step 2: Idea Expansion → ChatGPT

Input:

- Approved ideas from Notion

Tool:

- ChatGPT (saved prompts)

SOP:

1. Paste 5–10 ideas into ChatGPT.
2. Use your **Master Idea Expansion prompt**.
3. Generate:
   - Hooks
   - Formats
   - Angles
   - Repurpose opportunities

Output:

Expanded ideas pasted back into Notion.

Checkpoint:

Human selects which ideas become scripts.

Step 3: Scriptwriting → ChatGPT + Human Edit

Input:

- Expanded idea + hook

Tool:

- ChatGPT

SOP:

1. Generate first draft using script prompts.
2. Edit for:
   - Brand voice
   - Clarity
   - Authentic phrasing
3. Keep scripts short and modular.

Checkpoint:

Script approved before recording.

Step 4: Recording → Assets Folder

Input:

- Approved script

Tool:

- Phone / camera
- Cloud storage (Google Drive)

SOP:

1. Record vertical video (9:16).
2. Use multiple short takes.
3. Name files consistently:
   - ***2025-01-Brand-Hook-01.mp4***

Checkpoint:

Files uploaded to ***/Assets/Raw***.

Step 5: Editing → CapCut Templates

Input:

- Raw video files

Tool:

- CapCut (free)

SOP:

1. Open template project.
2. Drop clips into placeholders.
3. Auto-generate captions.
4. Add light B-roll and motion text.

Output:

Final video exported to ***/Assets/Final***.

Checkpoint:

Visual and pacing review.

Step 6: Thumbnails & Captions → Canva + ChatGPT

Input:

- Final video

Tools:

- Canva
- ChatGPT

SOP:

1. Ask ChatGPT for 5 headline options.
2. Select one headline.
3. Drop into Canva thumbnail template.
4. Generate caption variations.

Checkpoint:

Final approval for brand consistency.

Step 7: Scheduling → Buffer / Zapier

Input:

- Final assets + captions

Tools:

- Buffer
- Zapier (optional)

SOP:

1. Upload content to Buffer.
2. Schedule per platform cadence.

3. Optional: automate Notion → Buffer drafts.

Checkpoint:

Scheduled and visible on calendar.

Step 8: Monitor Engagement

Input:

- Live post

Tools:

- Native platform
- Notion CRM
- ChatGPT drafts

SOP:

1. Collect comments daily.
2. Use AI to draft replies.
3. Human posts final responses.

Checkpoint:

Engagement logged and categorized.

17.2 Roles: Who Does What

Even solo creators wear three hats.

AI Role

- Idea expansion
- Draft scripts
- Captions
- Repurposing

- Analytics summaries

Human Role

- Brand voice
- Final decisions
- Sensitive replies
- Strategic direction

Assistant Role (Optional)

- Uploading
- Scheduling
- Basic engagement
- Asset organization

Rule:

AI never publishes directly.
Humans always approve.

Action Steps — Chapter 17

- Build your pipeline as a Notion board
- Assign a role to every step
- Add a **"Ready for Next Step"** status to prevent stalls

Chapter 18 — AI Automation for Personal Brands

Personal brands are content goldmines —if captured correctly.

Most of your best content already exists in:

- Calls
- Conversations
- Coaching sessions
- Speaking moments

Automation lets you **extract value without re-recording**.

18.1 Coach Workflow Example

Input:

Weekly coaching call (Zoom, Meet, etc.)

SOP:

1. Record the call.
2. Transcribe using CapCut or free transcription.
3. Paste transcript into ChatGPT.

Prompt Objective:

Extract:

- Core insights
- Teachings

- Memorable quotes

Outputs:

- 4 short-form reels
- 1 LinkedIn article
- 1 newsletter excerpt

Checkpoint:

Human selects strongest moments.

Action Steps — Chapter 18

- Take your next call
- Generate 3 content pieces
- Publish one within 48 hours

Chapter 19 — AI Automation for Businesses

Businesses use the same system—but different inputs.

19.1 Niche Examples

<u>**E-Commerce**</u>

Input:

Product demo video

Outputs:

- 10 short clips
- 3 Instagram carousels
- 1 email campaign

Automation Focus:

Highlight features, benefits, objections.

Local Restaurant

Input:

Daily specials + atmosphere

Outputs:

- Stories
- Reels
- Auto-replies for hours and reservations

Automation Focus:

Consistency and responsiveness.

Action Steps — Chapter 19

- Choose one business type
- Map one week of content using the system
- Identify repeatable inputs

Chapter 20 — Scaling With Zero Budget

Scaling is not buying tools.

Scaling is **removing friction**.

20.1 When to Stay Free vs Upgrade

Upgrade only when:

- You hit scheduling limits
- Manual time > subscription cost
- Automation saves real hours

Rule:

- Process first.

- Tools second.

Action Steps — Chapter 20

1. Track hours saved per month.
2. Multiply by your hourly rate.
3. Upgrade only if ROI is clear.

Final Thought for PART V

When systems are clear, creativity becomes safe.

You are no longer guessing what to do next.
You are operating a machine that compounds.

In the next section, you'll get the **exact prompts, templates, and blueprints** that power everything you just built.

PART VI — TEMPLATES, PROMPTS & BLUEPRINTS

The Execution Engine

Everything you've built so far—systems, workflows, automation—depends on one thing: inputs.

This section gives you those inputs.

Part VI is not meant to be read once and forgotten. It is meant to be **opened daily**, copied freely, and adapted endlessly. These prompts, templates, and checklists are the mechanical levers that keep your social media automation system running even when time, energy, or creativity is low.

If earlier parts taught you how to build the machine, this part is the fuel.

Your Copy-Paste Control Panel

Everything up to this point has taught you *how the system works*.

This section is where you **run it**.

Part VI exists so you never have to start from a blank page again. It is not theory, strategy, or inspiration. It is a **working toolbox**—built to be copied, pasted, customized, and reused as often as you like.

If earlier parts of the book showed you *why* automation matters and *how* to build it, this part gives you the **exact inputs** that make the system move.

How to Use This Section

Think of **Part VI** as your **operating system**:

- **Prompts** are your engines
- **Calendars** are your pacing controls
- **Checklists** are your safety rails
- **Troubleshooting guides** are your reset buttons

You can:

- Jump straight to a prompt when you're stuck
- Drop a calendar into Notion or Google Sheets
- Run a checklist when motivation is low
- Diagnose performance issues without guessing

You do **not** need to read this section in order. Use it like a reference manual.

A Rule for Maximum Results

Prompts work best when:

1. You customize the variables (brand, voice, audience)
2. You reuse them consistently
3. You refine them based on performance

These are **starter prompts**, not magic spells. The real leverage comes from repetition and iteration.

What You'll Find in This Section

Chapter 21 — High-Performing Prompts Library

Battle-tested prompts for:

- Idea generation
- Scriptwriting
- Captions and hashtags
- Repurposing long-form content
- Turning analytics into insights

These are designed to work on **free AI tools** and are written to minimize fluff and maximize usable output.

Chapter 22 — Ready-to-Use Posting Calendars

Simple 30-day structures that remove decision fatigue while maintaining consistency and variety. You'll know exactly what to post—and why—every week.

Chapter 23 — Checklists (Daily / Weekly / Monthly)

Execution over motivation. These checklists keep your system running even on busy or low-energy days.

Chapter 24 — Troubleshooting Guide

When engagement drops, reach stalls, or content starts feeling stale, this chapter helps you diagnose the problem and apply targeted fixes—without panic or overhauls.

The Promise of Part VI

If you do nothing else:

- Copy one prompt

- Follow one calendar
- Complete one checklist

You will still publish more consistently, with less effort, than most creators and businesses online.

This section exists to **remove friction, reduce thinking,** and **turn action into habit**.

When you're ready, start with Chapter 21 and copy your first prompt.

That's all it takes to restart the machine.

Chapter 21 — High-Performing Prompts Library (Copy-Paste Ready)

Prompts are instructions. Weak instructions produce vague output. Strong instructions produce assets you can publish.

This chapter provides **tested prompt frameworks** that work across platforms and free AI tools. Each prompt includes:

- When to use it
- How to customize it
- What to do with the output

21.1 Master Idea Generator

Purpose:

To instantly generate a month's worth of structured content ideas from a single topic.

When to use:

- Weekly idea batching
- Content planning sessions
- When your idea list runs dry

Prompt (Copy & Paste):

I am {brand_name}.
My voice: {3 adjectives}.
My audience: {audience description}.

Produce 30 content ideas for {platform} about {topic}.

For each idea include:
1) A 1-line hook
2) Suggested format (short video, carousel, long post)

3) Estimated length
4) Three supporting bullet points
5) Repurpose actions for at least two other platforms

How to use (Step-by-Step):

1. Replace the variables with your brand details.
2. Run the prompt in ChatGPT.
3. Scan for ideas that:
   - Address pain points
   - Teach something specific
   - Trigger curiosity
4. Save the top 10 ideas into your Notion content database.
5. Mark them as **"Ready for Script."**

Pro Tip:

Run this prompt twice with slightly different audience descriptions to widen your content angles.

21.2 Script Prompt for a 45-Second Reel

Purpose:

To turn a single hook into a structured, scroll-stopping video script.

When to use:

- Reels, TikTok, Shorts
- Batch recording days

Prompt:

Write a 45-second script for a reel.

Hook: {hook}

Requirements:
- Conversational tone
- Three short scenes
- Directions for visuals or cutaways
- Suggested text overlays
- CTA: "Save and follow"
- Sentences under 12 words

How to use:

1. Paste in one hook from your idea list.
2. Review for:
   - Natural speech
   - Clear pacing
   - Strong opening sentence
3. Edit lightly to add personal phrasing.
4. Use the script exactly as written when recording.

Output Usage:

- Scene directions → editing guide
- Text overlays → captions or on-screen text
- CTA → consistent engagement driver

21.3 Caption + Hashtag Generator

Purpose:

To eliminate caption fatigue while still sounding human.

Prompt:

Create 3 caption variations (short, medium, long) for this post:
{paste script or summary}

Include:
- 10 relevant hashtags
- A suggested first comment with 10 additional hashtags
- Appropriate emojis

How to use:

1. Paste the final script or post summary.
2. Choose one caption length based on platform:
   - Short → TikTok
   - Medium → Instagram
   - Long → LinkedIn
3. Paste hashtags into caption or first comment.
4. Save all variations in Notion for A/B testing.

21.4 Repurpose Prompt (The Content Multiplier)

Purpose:

To turn one long-form asset into multiple platform-specific pieces.

Prompt:

Here is a transcript:
{paste transcript}

Tasks:
1) Split into 5 short scripts (30–45s) for reels with hooks and CTAs
2) Create 6 tweet-sized quotes
3) Write a 500-word LinkedIn post with a strong opening hook

How to use:

1. Paste transcript from CapCut or VEED.

2. Save each output into your content database.
3. Assign formats and publish dates.
4. Link all outputs back to the original content.

21.5 Analytics Insight Prompt

Purpose:

To turn raw numbers into decisions.

Prompt:

Here are my weekly metrics:
{paste table}

Write:
- A 4-sentence performance summary
- 3 testable hypotheses for next week

How to use:

1. Paste metrics from Google Sheets.
2. Copy the summary into your weekly report.
3. Use hypotheses to guide next week's content tests.

Chapter 22 — Ready-to-Use Posting Calendars

Consistency beats creativity when systems are involved. These calendars remove daily decision-making.

22.1 The Simple 30-Day Posting Plan

Weekly Structure:

- **Monday:** Short tutorial
- **Wednesday:** Carousel or value post
- **Friday**: Personal story + CTA
- **Daily:** 1–3 Stories (optional)

Weekly Themes:

- **Week 1**: Brand foundations & core pain point
- **Week 2**: Case studies & social proof
- **Week 3**: Tutorials & micro-training
- **Week 4**: Repurpose top content + AMA

How to implement:

1. Pre-assign formats to each weekday.
2. Use prompts from **Chapter 21** to fill content.
3. Schedule everything one week in advance.

22.2 Example Day Template

Post:

- 60-second tutorial video (scripted)

Caption:

- Long-form caption with CTA

Stories:

- 3 behind-the-scenes clips:
  - Setup
  - Process
  - Result

Chapter 23 — Execution Checklists

Checklists replace motivation with momentum.

23.1 Daily Checklist (10–15 minutes)

- Review notifications (respond or draft replies)
- Confirm scheduled post went live
- Capture 3 new ideas in Notion

23.2 Weekly Checklist (60–90 minutes)

- Batch record or edit content

- Repurpose one long-form asset
- Pull metrics and run analytics prompt

23.3 Monthly Checklist (90–120 minutes)

- Audit top 10 posts
- Identify winning hooks and formats
- Refresh templates and prompts
- Update SOPs based on friction points

Chapter 24 — Troubleshooting Guide

When results dip, don't panic—diagnose.

24.1 Low Engagement

Symptoms:

- Low saves, shares, comments

Fixes:

- Rewrite hooks for curiosity
- Test different posting times
- Improve thumbnail clarity

24.2 Shadowban Fears

Symptoms:

- Sudden drop in reach

Fixes:

- Reduce automation frequency
- Add manual replies
- Avoid repetitive captions

24.3 Content Fatigue

Symptoms:

- Content feels repetitive
- Audience disengages

Fixes:

- Add personal stories
- Use user questions as content
- Rotate formats weekly

Final Note for Part VI

You do not need more tools.
You need **repeatable inputs**.

If you consistently:

- Use these prompts
- Follow these calendars
- Run these checklists

Your content system will run—even on days you don't feel creative.

This is how automation becomes sustainable growth.

Chapter 25: Master System Map — How All SOPs Connect

The **Master System Map** is the single most important page in this book.

Instead of thinking in isolated tasks—"make a post," "edit a video," "reply to comments"—this map shows the **entire automation ecosystem** from idea to growth.

If you understand this map, everything else becomes easier.

Most people fail at social media not because they lack ideas, tools, or effort—but because they see content creation as **disconnected tasks**:

- "I need to post today."

- “I should reply to comments.”
- “I should make a reel.”
- “I should check analytics.”

That thinking creates burnout, inconsistency, and chaos.

The **Master System Map** replaces task-based thinking with **system-based thinking**.

It shows how **every Standard Operating Procedure (SOP) in this book connects into one continuous, repeatable workflow**—from idea to growth, from content to conversion, from chaos to control.

This chapter will teach you how to *read, use,* and *build* your business around this one-page system.

What the Master System Map Is (and Is Not)

The Master System Map is:

- A **bird's-eye blueprint** of your entire content operation
- A visual representation of **how work flows**, not how tools work
- A reference you can return to whenever you feel overwhelmed

The Master System Map is **not**:

- A detailed tutorial (those live in individual SOPs)
- A rigid workflow (you can customize tools without breaking the system)
- A list of apps (apps change; systems endure)

Think of it like an airport map.
You don't see every screw in the airplane—you see how terminals, gates, security, and runways connect.

The Five Layers of the Master System Map

The map is organized into **five stacked layers**, each flowing into the next.

Nothing stands alone.
Nothing is wasted.
Everything feeds forward.

Layer 1: Input — Where Content Is Born

Every system begins with raw material.

Your input layer answers one question:

"Where do ideas come from?"

Instead of relying on inspiration, this system **engineers inputs** from predictable sources.

Core Input Sources

1. Idea Capture (Notion Mobile or Notes App)

Ideas should be captured the moment they appear, not when you sit down to create.

Examples:

- A thought during a walk
- A lesson from a client call
- A mistake you just made

- A question someone asked you

SOP Connection: Idea Capture SOP

2. Long-Form Content

One long-form asset can fuel weeks of short-form content.

Examples:

- YouTube videos
- Podcast episodes
- Blog articles
- Workshops or live streams

This is the foundation of leverage.

SOP Connection: Long-Form to Short-Form SOP

3. Customer Questions, Comments, and DMs

Your audience tells you exactly what to create—if you listen.

Examples:

- Repeated questions
- Objections before buying
- Confusion points
- Emotional pain points

SOP Connection: Audience Mining SOP

4. Trends and Competitor Insights

Trends are not copied—they are translated into your voice.

Examples:

- Trending audio formats
- Popular hooks
- Viral content structures

SOP Connection: Trend Monitoring SOP

All of these inputs flow into a **single idea pool**.

Layer 2: Processing — The AI-Assisted Engine

This is where raw ideas become publishable assets.

The processing layer answers:

“How do we turn ideas into content efficiently?”

This is the heart of automation.

The AI Content Machine

Once an idea enters the system, it passes through structured transformation.

1. Idea Expansion (ChatGPT)

A single idea becomes multiple angles.

- Educational
- Story-based
- Opinionated
- Tactical

SOP Connection: Idea Expansion Prompt Library

2. Scriptwriting & Caption Drafting

AI creates:

- Short-form video scripts
- Carousel copy
- Long-form captions
- CTA variations

You review, refine, and approve.

SOP Connection: Script & Caption SOP

3. Visual Creation (Canva)

Templates ensure speed and brand consistency.

Examples:

- Carousel slides
- Reel covers
- Quote graphics

SOP Connection: Visual Template SOP

4. Video Editing (CapCut)

AI-assisted editing reduces friction.

Examples:

- Auto captions
- Jump cuts
- Format resizing

SOP Connection: Short-Form Video SOP

5. Repurposing Logic (1→15 Method)

One piece of content becomes many.

Examples:

- 1 long video → 5 reels → 5 stories → 5 quote posts

SOP Connection: Repurposing SOP

Once processed, content is ready for distribution.

Layer 3: Output — Publishing at Scale

This layer answers:

"How does content get published consistently without manual effort?"

Publishing & Scheduling

1. Scheduled Posts

Content is queued in advance using free tools.

Examples:

- Buffer
- Metricool

SOP Connection: Scheduling SOP

2. Multi-Platform Distribution

The same content is adapted for:

- Instagram
- TikTok
- LinkedIn

- YouTube Shorts

SOP Connection: Platform Adaptation SOP

3. Format Variety

Your feed stays dynamic without extra work.

Formats include:

- Stories
- Reels
- Carousels
- Static posts

Once content is live, the system shifts focus from publishing to people.

Layer 4: Engagement & Growth — Where Trust Is Built

Posting content is only half the game.

This layer answers:

“How do we turn attention into relationships?”

Engagement Workflow

1. Comment Replies

AI drafts responses, humans approve.

- Faster replies
- Consistent tone
- No emotional burnout

SOP Connection: Comment Management SOP

2. DM Automation & CRM Tracking

Not all DMs are equal.

Leads are:

- Tagged
- Categorized
- Followed up

SOP Connection: DM & CRM SOP

3. Community Management

Engagement is intentional, not reactive.

Examples:

- Pinning comments

- Highlighting users
- Starting conversations

All engagement produces **data**.

Layer 5: Analytics & Feedback Loop — How the System Improves

This layer answers:

"How does the system get better over time?"

Measurement & Optimization

1. Weekly Metrics Collection

- Reach

- Saves
- Shares
- Follows
- Comments

SOP Connection: Metrics SOP

2. AI-Generated Insights

AI identifies:

- What worked
- What failed
- What patterns repeat

SOP Connection: Analytics Prompt SOP

3. Optimization Decisions

Based on data:

- Double down on winners
- Kill low performers
- Test new hooks

Insights feed back into the **Input Layer**, closing the loop.

Why the Master System Map Matters

This map does four critical things:

1. **Turns dozens of SOPs into one mental model**

   You stop memorizing tasks and start understanding flow.

2. **Prevents overwhelm**

You always know what comes next.

3. **Enables delegation and automation**

   You can assign entire layers—not just tasks.

4. **Reveals bottlenecks instantly**

   If growth slows, you know exactly where to look.

How to Use This Map Daily

- Review it when building your weekly plan
- Reference it when creating or updating SOPs
- Share it with contractors or team members
- Use it as your "north star" when adding new tools

Final Thought

Most creators obsess over individual machines:

- Better prompts
- Better editing
- Better hooks

But businesses are built by **factories**, not machines.

The **Master System Map** is the blueprint of your factory.

Everything else in this book exists to support it.

MASTER SYSTEM MAP
— How All SOPs Connect

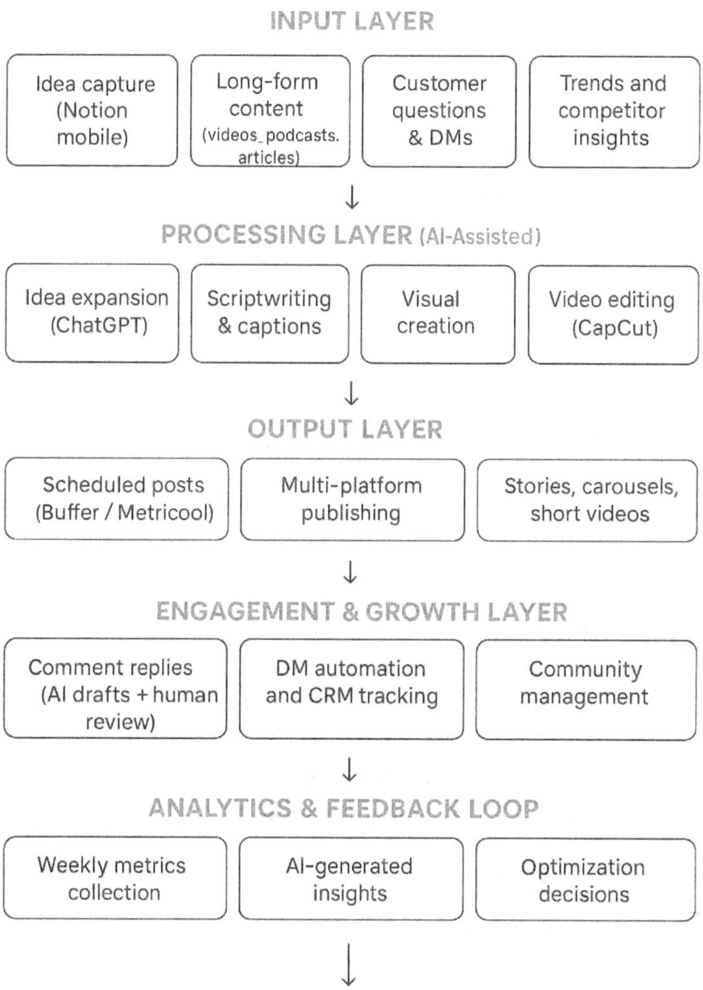

Chapter 26: The Complete AI Prompt Library

BRAND VOICE PROMPTS

Create/Refine Your Brand Voice

Prompt:

"Analyze my brand and create a clear brand voice description using these elements: tone, style, pacing, vocabulary, emotional intent, and how I speak to my audience.

Here is my brand information:

- *3 core messages: {insert}*

- *Audience: {insert}*
- *My writing sample: {paste 1–3 paragraphs}*

Create a Brand Voice Summary I can reuse."

Brand Voice Transformation

Prompt:

"Rewrite the following text in my brand voice (see voice description below). Keep the meaning the same but match tone, pacing, and vocabulary.
Brand voice: {insert}
Text: {insert}"

Brand Voice Consistency Check

Prompt:

"Review the following post for consistency with my brand voice. Suggest improvements to wording, tone, and clarity:
{paste post}"

CONTENT IDEA PROMPTS

30-Day Content Idea Generator

Prompt:

"Based on my brand voice and audience pain points, create a list of 30 high-quality content ideas for social media.
Brand messages: {insert}
Pain points: {insert}

Platform: {IG/TikTok/LinkedIn/etc}. Format: bullet list + recommended content type (reel, carousel, post).”

Idea Expansion (10 Angles Prompt)

Prompt:

“Take this topic—{topic}—and generate 10 different content angles (instructional, motivational, myth-busting, storytelling, mistakes, templates, etc.).”

Best-of Series Prompt

Prompt:

“Generate a ‘Top 10 Things You Need to Know About {topic}’ list with 1–2

sentence explanations for each item."

HOOK & HEADLINE PROMPTS

Viral Hook Generator

Prompt:

"Give me 20 high-impact hooks for a 30–60 second video about {topic}. Include curiosity hooks, contrarian hooks, and emotional hooks."

Carousel Headline Prompt

Prompt:

"Create 10 punchy carousel titles about {topic} written for Instagram. Make them short, bold, and curiosity-driven."

LinkedIn Headline Prompt

Prompt:

"Write 10 bold, scroll-stopping LinkedIn post headlines about {topic}. Tone: professional, confident, insight-driven."

CAPTION & COPYWRITING PROMPTS

Multi-Version Caption Prompt

Prompt:

***"Write 3 caption variations (short, medium, long) for this post concept: {insert}.
Include a CTA and 8–12 relevant hashtags."***

Storytelling Caption Prompt

Prompt:

"Write a storytelling-style caption that follows this structure:

- ***Hook***
- ***Setup***
- ***Conflict***
- ***Insight***
- ***CTA***

***Topic: {insert}
Tone: {brand voice}."***

Micro-Copy / Tweet Prompts

Prompt:

"Write 10 short punchy lines (Tweet/ X-style content) about {topic}. Keep each under 240 characters."

SCRIPTWRITING PROMPTS

Short-Form Script Prompt (30–45 sec)

Prompt:

"Write a 3-scene script for a 30–45 second short-form video about {topic}.
Structure:
• Scene 1: Hook (2–3 seconds)

• Scene 2: Value (3 points)
• Scene 3: CTA
Tone: {brand voice}."

Long-Form Script Prompt (YouTube/Live)

Prompt:

"Write a 3–5 minute script for a YouTube video about {topic}.
Structure:

1. ***Hook***
2. ***Introduce the problem***
3. ***Teach 3–5 lessons***
4. ***Conclusion + CTA."***

B-Roll Suggestions Prompt

Prompt:

"Suggest 10 B-roll ideas for a reel about {topic}. Include options I can shoot on my phone + stock footage ideas."

REPURPOSING PROMPTS

Repurpose One Video Into 10 Posts

Prompt:

"Take the transcript below and repurpose it into 10 different content formats:
- *3 reels*
- *2 carousels*
- *2 tweets*
- *1 LinkedIn post*
- *1 quote graphic*

• 1 short caption
Transcript: {insert}"

Turn Long-Form Into Short Clips

Prompt:

"Identify 10–15 timestamps from this long video that would make strong short clips. Include suggested hooks for each:
Transcript/video summary: {insert}"

Multi-Platform Rewrite

Prompt:

"Rewrite this idea for 5 platforms: IG, TikTok, FB, LinkedIn, X.
Keep meaning the same; change tone + format for each.

Idea: {insert}"

ENGAGEMENT & COMMUNITY PROMPTS

Comment Reply Generator

Prompt:

"Write 5 friendly responses in my brand voice to this comment: {insert}."

DM Auto-Responder (Use Cautiously)

Prompt:

"Write a helpful, respectful auto-response for incoming DMs about {topic}.
Tone: warm, helpful, human.
Purpose: route them to resources or invite conversation."

Community Questions Prompt

Prompt:

"Give me 10 questions I can ask my audience to increase engagement around {topic}. Make them fun and easy to answer."

ANALYTICS & OPTIMIZATION PROMPTS

Post Performance Analysis

Prompt:

"Analyze the following post's performance metrics and provide:
• 3 insights
• Why it worked or didn't work
• 3 recommendations to improve future posts
Metrics: {insert}
Caption/Content: {insert}"

Weekly Content Review

Prompt:

"Here are my last 7 posts. Summarize patterns and give me:
• What to double down on
• What to stop doing
• 5 ideas to try next week
Data: {insert}"

Data-Driven Headlines Prompt

Prompt:

"Based on my top-performing posts, create 10 new headlines or hooks that align with what historically performs best.
Top-performing examples: {insert}"

SYSTEM-BUILDING PROMPTS

SOP Creation Prompt

Prompt:

"Write a step-by-step SOP for {process} using clear numbered instructions and checkboxes."

Workflow Mapping Prompt

Prompt:

***"Help me create a workflow for my content production using this sequence:
Idea → Draft → Visual → Edit → Schedule → Publish → Repurpose → Analyze
Describe each stage and the tools used."***

30-Day Content Calendar Prompt

Prompt:

***"Generate a 30-day content calendar for {platform}.
Include:***

- ***Post type***
- ***Hook***
- ***Topic***
- ***CTA***
- ***Suggested visual"***

Chapter 27: The Social Media Automation Prompt Pact

Below is a complete, ready-to-use prompt library and operating system for ideation, creation, repurposing, scheduling, analytics, and engagement to run your entire content machine with AI.

You can paste any section directly into ChatGPT (or another LLM) and it will function as a reusable "automation module."

BRAND FOUNDATION PROMPTS

(Use these once, refine them quarterly.)

Brand Voice Builder

Prompt:

Act as my Brand Voice Architect. Analyze the following information and create a brand voice profile including Tone, Syntax, Vocabulary, Pacing, Do’s, Don’ts, and Signature Phrases.

Target audience: [describe]
Core messages: [list]
Personality traits: [list]
Competitors: [list]

Deliver my Brand Voice Blueprint.

Audience Pain-Point Mapper

Prompt:

Analyze my ideal audience and produce a list of:
- *10 core desire statements*
- *10 fears*
- *10 frustrations*
- *10 daily obstacles*
- *10 identity-level aspirations*

Present them in a table with content angles for each.

Brand Positioning Story

Prompt:

Convert my brand mission into a clean "Origin → Struggle → Shift → Solution → Proof" narrative.
Mission: [insert]
Unique value: [insert]

Deliver 3 versions:
- *Short (30 seconds)*
- *Medium (2 minutes)*

• Long (hero story)

IDEATION PROMPTS (DAILY/ WEEKLY)

100-Piece Content Idea Explosion

Prompt:

Using my brand voice and audience profile, generate:
• 20 educational ideas
• 20 myth-busting ideas
• 20 inspirational ideas
• 20 controversial opinions
• 20 personal stories

Each idea must fit short-form video.

Trend Hijack Scanner

Prompt:

Based on today's trends in [platform], give me:
- *5 trend formats I should use*
- *Scripts for each*
- *Hooks optimized for 3 seconds*
- *Filming instructions*

Keep the tone aligned with my brand.

Pain-Point to Post Generator

Prompt:

Here are my audience's top 5 pain points:
[list]

Turn each pain point into:
- *A short-form video idea*

• A story-based carousel
• A 1-paragraph LinkedIn post
• A newsletter opening hook

Deliver in template form.

CONTENT CREATION PROMPTS

Hook Factory

Prompt:

Create 20 variations of short-form video hooks using these formulas:
• Curiosity
• Pattern break
• Fear of loss
• Status boost
• Direct promise

Topic: [insert]

Script Generator

Prompt:

Write a 45–60 second video script.
Structure:

- ***Hook***
- ***Problem***
- ***Explanation***
- ***Mini case study***
- ***CTA***

Topic: [insert].

Caption Generator

Prompt:

Write 3 captions for the attached script:
• Short (under 120 characters)
• Medium (story style)
• Long (value-based, saves/shares focus)

Include 8 relevant hashtags.

Carousel Creator

Prompt:

Turn the following topic into a 7-slide carousel.
• Slide 1: Big hook
• Slides 2–6: Value
• Slide 7: CTA

Topic: [insert].

REPURPOSING PROMPTS

Omnichannel Repurposing Engine

Prompt:

Take this long-form text and convert it into:
• 1 YouTube video outline
• 3 TikTok/Reels scripts
• 1 LinkedIn post
• 2 tweets
• 1 carousel outline
• 1 email newsletter

Keep tone consistent across formats.

Short → Long Expansion

Prompt:

Take this 30-second script and expand it into a 500–800 word article. Preserve voice. Provide section headers.

Long → Micro Content Shards

Prompt:

Break this long-form post into 15 micro content pieces:

- *Hooks*
- *One-liners*
- *Quotes*
- *Mini-lessons*

Topic: [insert long text].

<u>AUTOMATION PROMPTS</u>

Scheduling Plan Builder

Prompt:

Based on my cadence (3 posts/week + 1 long-form/month), create a 30-day content schedule including:

- ***Post type***
- ***Hook***
- ***Platform***
- ***CTA***
- ***Repurpose notes***

Auto-Response DM Scripts

Prompt:

Generate:

• 3 "thank you for following" DM sequences
• 3 sales funnel DM sequences
• 3 FAQ response templates

Tone must feel human and conversational.

Comment Engine

Prompt:

Create 20 customizable, non-generic comment templates for:
• Engaging with followers
• Engaging with creators
• Community building

Tone: warm + value-first.

ANALYTICS & OPTIMIZATION PROMPTS

Performance Analyzer

Prompt:

Analyze this data (views, watch time, saves, shares) and answer:
- *What worked?*
- *Why?*
- *What should be repeated?*
- *What should be changed?*
- *What new hypotheses should we test?*

Then give me 5 content ideas based on the findings.

Hook Split-Test Lab

Prompt:

Create 10 new hook variations for this post:
[paste text]

Each must be under 8 words.

Content Calendar Optimization

Prompt:

Redesign my content calendar to prioritize top-performing formats, topics, and post types using a 70/20/10 model:
- *70% proven content*
- *20% experimental*
- *10% trending*

Output the next 30 days.

ADVANCED PROMPTS (PRO MODE)

AI Co-Creator Mode

Prompt:

For this project, you are my AI Co-Creator.
Your role: challenge my assumptions, improve my ideas, and push creativity without losing my brand voice.

Each idea you give me must come with:
- *Why it works*
- *How it fits the algorithm*
- *My unique angle*

Topic: [insert].

The "One Big Idea" Filter

Prompt:

Evaluate my idea and refine it until it becomes one strong, clean, viral-ready concept:
[paste idea]

Provide:
- *A shorter version*
- *A punchier version*
- *A more emotional version*
- *A more contrarian version*

Viral Structure Breakdown

Prompt:

Break down this viral post into structural elements:
- *Hook*
- *Stakes*

• *Tension*
• *Payoff*
• *CTA*

Then rewrite it using my brand voice.

<u>DONE-FOR-YOU PACKS</u>

These are “plug and go” sequences.

7-Day Kickstart Pack

Prompt:

Create a 7-day content plan with scripts, captions, hashtags, and repurposing instructions.
Focus: fast growth + audience resonance.

Tone: authentic, authority, approachable.

30-Day Authority Builder

Prompt:

Create a 30-day plan that positions me as an expert, including:

- *8 deep-dive posts*
- *8 how-to videos*
- *8 myths debunked*
- *6 personal stories*

Make the distribution platform-specific.

90-Day Social Media Automation System

Prompt:

Build a 90-day end-to-end automated content system based on:

- *My brand voice*
- *My cadence*
- *My niche*

Include:

- *Weekly workflow*
- *Daily tasks*
- *Automation tools*
- *Repurposing plan*
- *Monthly metrics review*
- *Templates for everything*

AFTERWORD

The System Is the Freedom

If you've reached this page, you've already done something most people never do: you stayed long enough to see the whole system.

Not the hacks.
Not the tools.
Not the trends.

The *system*.

This book was never about posting more. It was about **thinking differently**—about content, time, energy, and leverage. Social media rewards consistency, but consistency is not a personality trait. It's a structural one.

When creators burn out, it's rarely because they lack talent. It's because they built everything on effort instead of architecture.

What you now have is architecture.

You've learned how to:

- Turn ideas into assets instead of one-off posts
- Use AI as a multiplier, not a crutch
- Separate creation from distribution
- Replace memory with documentation
- Replace stress with workflows
- Replace guesswork with feedback loops

That's not social media marketing.

That's *systems thinking applied to visibility*.

Automation Is Not the Goal

Freedom is.

Automation doesn't exist to remove you from your brand. It exists to remove friction so you can show up where it matters most—your voice, your perspective, your relationships.

The best-performing content online still feels human.
The difference is that behind the scenes, it's **engineered**.

You now understand something most people won't for years:

- Creativity scales when structure exists

- Growth accelerates when decisions are repeatable
- Consistency becomes easy when systems carry the weight

Start Small. Stay Relentless.

You don't need to implement everything at once.

Pick one SOP.
Run it for 30 days.
Refine it.
Then add the next.

Momentum compounds quietly.

A single well-run system will outperform ten scattered efforts every time.

The Quiet Advantage

Most creators will continue:

- Posting manually
- Guessing what works
- Chasing algorithms
- Burning weekends for content

You won't.

You'll be building assets.
You'll be reading dashboards.
You'll be improving processes.
You'll be thinking like an operator, not a poster.

That is the quiet advantage.

Final Thought

Trends will change.
Platforms will shift.
Tools will evolve.

But **systems endure**.

When attention becomes chaotic, the people with structure win.
When effort becomes exhausting, the people with leverage survive.
When competition gets louder, the people with clarity stand out.

You now have the map.
You now have the tools.
You now have the system.

Build it once.
Run it calmly.
Improve it endlessly.

— Andy Hai Dinh

APPENDICES

These appendices exist to remove friction.

No theory.
No storytelling.
No motivation.

This section is where execution happens.

Use it to:

- Clarify terminology
- Quickly choose the right tools
- Copy proven templates
- Follow a concrete 30-day rollout plan
- Operate ethically and sustainably with AI

Bookmark this section. Print it if needed. Come back to it often.

Appendix A — Glossary of Essential AI & Automation Terms

This glossary defines key terms **as they are used in this book**, not as abstract technical concepts.

Prompt

A written instruction you give an AI tool that defines what to produce, how to produce it, and in what style. A good prompt replaces guesswork with structure.

Model

The underlying AI engine that processes prompts and generates outputs. Think of it as the “brain” behind tools like ChatGPT.

TTS (Text-to-Speech)

Technology that converts written text into spoken audio. Used for voiceovers, narration, and accessibility.

Transcription

The conversion of audio or video into written text. This is the foundation of repurposing long-form content.

Repurposing

The systematic transformation of one piece of content into multiple formats across platforms (e.g., one video → many posts).

KPI (Key Performance Indicator)

A metric that measures success toward a goal, such as engagement rate, saves, click-throughs, or follower growth.

Appendix B — Tools Cheat Sheet (Free or Free-Tier)

Use this as a quick-reference guide when setting up or troubleshooting your system.

ChatGPT

- Idea expansion
- Scriptwriting
- Caption drafting
- Comment & DM reply drafts

- Analytics summaries
- Repurposing logic

Primary Role: Brain and writing assistant

Notion

- Idea capture
- Content calendar
- CRM for DMs and leads
- SOP documentation
- Prompt libraries

Primary Role: Central command center

Canva

- Carousel design

- Thumbnails
- Brand templates
- Quote graphics

Primary Role: Visual consistency at speed

CapCut

- Short-form video editing
- Auto-captions
- Jump cuts
- Format resizing

Primary Role: Fast, repeatable video production

Buffer / Metricool

- Scheduling posts
- Multi-platform publishing
- Basic analytics

Primary Role: Distribution engine

Google Sheets

- Analytics tracking
- Growth calculations
- Weekly and monthly reports

Primary Role: Data organization and insight

Zapier (Free Tier)

- Automate simple handoffs
- Connect Notion → scheduling tools

Primary Role: Reducing manual steps

Appendix C — Example SOPs & Templates (Copy / Paste)

1. Notion Content & CRM Database Template

Database Fields

- Content Title
- Platform
- Content Type (Reel, Carousel, Story, Post)
- Status (Idea / Draft / Scheduled / Posted)
- Hook

- Caption Draft
- Asset Link
- Scheduled Date
- Performance Notes

CRM-Specific Fields

- Lead Name
- Platform
- First Touch Date
- Interest Level (Cold / Warm / Hot)
- Tags
- Conversation Snippets
- Last Contacted
- Next Action

2. Google Sheets — Weekly Growth Formulas

Example Columns

- Date
- Followers
- Impressions
- Reach
- Engagements

Growth Rate Formula

=(B2-B1)/B1

Engagement Rate

=Engagements/Reach

Weekly Summary Prompt (Paste into ChatGPT)
"Here are this week's metrics: [paste table]. Write a 4-sentence performance summary and suggest three optimization tests for next week."

3. Buffer CSV Upload Template (Example)

Date	Time	Message	Link	Image URL
2025-01-05	09:00	3 mistakes killing your reach		image.jpg

Use this format to batch-upload posts instead of scheduling manually.

Appendix D — 30-Day Action Plan (Step-by-Step)

This plan assumes **1 primary platform** and **no paid tools**.

Week 1 — Foundation & Setup

Day 1

- Choose one platform
- Decide posting cadence (3–5x/week)
- Create Notion workspace
- Create Brand Prompts document

Day 2

- Sign up for Canva, CapCut, Buffer, Zapier
- Create folder structure:
  - /Ideas
  - /Scripts
  - /Assets
  - /Posted

Day 3

- Run the Master Idea Generator
- Generate 30 content ideas
- Store them in Notion

Day 4

- Select top 10 ideas
- Create scripts using the Reel Script prompt

Day 5

- Design 3 reusable Canva templates

Day 6

- Record 3 short videos
- Record 1 long-form video

Day 7

- Edit one video in CapCut
- Create thumbnail
- Schedule first post

Week 2 — Production & Repurposing

Days 8–10

- Batch-edit remaining videos
- Export captions and thumbnails

Day 11

- Publish scheduled posts
- Repurpose long video into 5 clips

Day 12

- Set up Zapier: Notion → Buffer

Day 13

- Create 2 carousels
- Schedule them

Day 14

- Pull mid-month metrics
- Generate ChatGPT performance summary

Week 3 — Audience & Engagement

Days 15–17

- Generate comment reply templates

- Respond to DMs with AI drafts + human review

Day 18

- Launch CTA (AMA, poll, or giveaway)

Days 19–20

- Repurpose UGC into content

Day 21

- Identify top 2 formats
- Increase output for those formats

Week 4 — Scale & Consolidate

Days 22–24

- Improve SOPs
- Finalize templates

Day 25

- Clean Notion workspace
- Link assets

Day 26

- Schedule next 30 days

Days 27–29

- A/B test captions or posting times

Day 30

- Create monthly report

- Write next-month hypothesis using ChatGPT

Appendix E — Final Notes, Tools & Ethics

Automation is a force multiplier—not a replacement for integrity.

Guiding Principles

- Disclose AI usage when required
- Keep humans in the loop for sensitive topics
- Avoid deceptive or spammy automation
- Use AI to scale *helpfulness*, not manipulation

If automation removes humanity, it will fail long-term.

If automation frees you to show up better, clearer, and more consistently—it becomes an advantage very few people will ever build correctly.

This appendix completes the system.

Everything you need to operate, scale, and sustain your social media engine now lives in your hands.

OTHER BOOKS BY THIS AUTHOR

•Acrylic and Dipping Powder - Product Knowledge and Applications (Published: 2023)

•The Nail Technician's Career Guide (Published: 2023)

•A Beginner's Guide to Trading - Stock and Forex TechnicalAnalysis (Published: 2025)

•WIN MORE, TRADE BETTER - A Practical Guide to Trading and Investing (Published: 2025)

•Trade Smart: The Essential Guide to Markets, Analyses & Strategies (Published: 2025)

•Modern Vietnamese Cuisine: The Best Home-Cooking Recipes (Published: 2025)

•Modern Vietnamese Cuisine 2: Family Meals For All Occasions" (Published: 2025)

•Modern Vietnamese Cuisine 3: Delicious Street Food (Published: 2025)

•AI for Everyday Success: Master the Tools That Supercharge Productivity and Unlock New Income Streams (Published: 2025)

•The Nail Salon Owner's Bible: A Complete Guide to Building and Growing a Successful Nail Business (Published: 2025)

•The Art of Connection: A Comprehensive Guide to Mindful and Ecstatic Sex (Published: 2025)

•The Married Mind: A Psychological Guide to Building a Lasting Partnership (Published: 2025)

•The Unshakeable Adult: A Modern Guide to Thriving Through Life's Challenges (Published: 2025)

•Achieving Financial Freedom: The Complete Guide to Building Wealth and Creating Lasting Passive Income (Published: 2025)

•Retire & Thrive: A Friendly (but Serious) Guide to Your Golden Years (Published: 2025)

•How To Survive An Alien Invasion: The essential guide to enduring the unthinkable (Published: 2025)

•A Prepper's Personal Security and Self-Defense Manual (Published: 2025)

•Survival Kit Mastery: A Practical Guide to Building Essential Gear Systems (Published: 2025)

•How to Build a Business That Runs Without You: The Systems, Mindsets, and Blueprints to Escape the Daily Grind and Build a Truly Valuable Company (Published: 2025)